T0003736

POWERFUL PRINCESSES

10 UNTOLD STORIES OF HISTORY'S BOLDEST HEROINES

ANGELA BUCKINGHAM

ILLUSTRATIONS BY ANNE YVONNE GILBERT

FOR THE CHILDREN I LOVE,
FROM ANGELA

FOR DANNY,
FROM YVONNE

Made with love by the team at

FIVE MILE

Michelle, Rocco, Jacqui, Graham, Claire, Sarah, Bridget, Tillie, Kate & Victoria

Five Mile,
the publishing division
of Regency Media
www.fivemile.com.au

First published 2020
This paperback edition published in 2023

Text copyright © Angela Buckingham, 2020
Illustrations copyright © Anne Yvonne Gilbert, 2020
Author photo by Jade Riviére.

All rights reserved. No part of this publication may be
reproduced, stored in a retrieval system, or transmitted in any
way or by any means, electronic, mechanical photocopying,
recording or otherwise, without the prior permission of the
publisher.

A catalogue record for this book is available from the National
Library of Australia

Printed in China 5 4 3 2 1

NATIONAL
LIBRARY
OF AUSTRALIA

THE PRINCESSES

Welcome

Swashbuckling ladies, daring girls and audacious grandmas – the ten women in this book show us that there are many different ways to be brave, and many different types of princess.

These princesses' stories are exciting, full of adventure and actually happened, unlike the princess fairytales I was told when I was about your age.

My childhood princess was always beautiful. She was the prize. The solution to her problem was usually to get married. Even with that predictable plot, we liked these princess fairytales because the books were filled with gorgeous illustrations and always ended with a 'happily ever after'.

Back then, there were lots of these stories about princesses and almost everyone knew them. So people shared an understanding of what a princess was. This one vision of the perfect princess was part of our shared imagination, along with dragons and witches. But unlike dragons and witches, this idea of the princess was also a sort of guide to how real girls were expected to behave.

Of course, princesses are not just characters in fairytales. Princesses pop up in our history books, the real stories of our past. Princesses appear in these stories much more often than other women like peasants, seamstresses and shopkeepers, though less often than kings, princes, barons and the odd queen.

Our history books usually tell us who princesses married and, more often than makes sense, what they wore! Maybe historians were influenced by the fairytales they read? But occasionally in a history book I've come across a story that hints of a princess who behaved in a most un-princess-like fashion. It is these real-life women who have inspired the true princess stories in this book.

We must ask who actually was a real princess? (I'm not talking about sticking peas under the mattress here.)

Historically, the title of 'princess' is European and typically describes females of a certain royal rank within a European royal family. But the heroines in this book come from all over the world.

Many women in these stories came from societies that don't use the word 'princess'. But, importantly, all the women in this collection were recognised as 'royal' because of the social position of their birth and their family's high status within their communities.

More importantly, these stories are about women who took action because they had a sense of responsibility or a sense of the rights that came with their special social status. The title 'princess' is given to all the women in this book from a position of respect. Implicit gratitude informs these tales. The more I research these women the more I admire them.

While this book is about real stories and research, it is also about imagination – your imagination, my imagination and our shared imagination. This exploration of powerful princesses must be an act of imagination, inspired by facts but not confined by them.

Dreaming what it felt like, looked like and smelt like to live as these women is one way to understand their worlds as well as their bravery and triumphs. Similarly, these stories are adventures, not morality tales. I did not write these stories to encourage you to be good. Rather, these princesses fire my imagination, and I hope they do the same for you.

This book is just the beginning. If you want to know more about these women's lives, please start your own research: go to a library or do an online search. It is important work. Many of these stories come from historical records that are not complete or were written by the princesses' enemies or are simply so old that much of the detail is uncertain.

Most of our history books are filled with the stories of men. We need more stories from women's history. For too long, many women and their stories were just not included in the official accounts of human past. For this reason many details of women's stories have been lost over time.

We need to find the historical clues that allow us to put these stories back together. So if I haven't included your favourite princess or if you find a new fact, please share it with me and those to whom you tell tales. That way we will all have richer stories and a better understanding of princesses. And that will change the way we imagine all princesses.

If we change the way we imagine princesses we break the idea that only the fairytale princess is perfect. And in doing that we create lots of ways that we can be the heroine or hero we want to be.

So enjoy,

Angela

Princess Map

The stories in this collection took place all over the world. The names of regions, countries and towns often change over time. The place names used in these stories are the names that would have been known to the people at the time of the story.

NORTH AMERICA ⑨

SOUTH AMERICA

1.
Aud

2.
Noor

3.
Ping Yang

4.
Te Puea

5.
Nzinga

6.
Alice

7.
Clotilda

8.
Asmau

9.
Lozen

10.
Elizabeth

Aud

Around 1150 years ago, Aud, mother of a Viking king, had to save her people after her son's defeat and death …

Aud weeps on the cold blue beach. It takes three men to lift her broken son onto the funeral pyre. He was a big man. They called him Thorstien the Red.

He was brutal in winning land from the Picts. He swept across their plains, took their cattle, burnt their houses and captured them as slaves. But then after many years, the Picts had their revenge. They paid some of Thorstien's soldiers to betray him.

The fire rages hotter and brighter, burning Thorstien's body to ashes. Aud cries with fear for what the Picts will do to her family now her son is dead.

After the battle, the victorious Picts shelter in their forts. They hide not from Aud's people but from winter. The clouds

hang low over the bare fields. The only creatures in the forest are prowling wolves. But Aud knows as soon as spring returns, the Picts will attack.

As the fire takes the spirits of dead warriors, Aud looks past the orange flames out at the black swelling sea. She stops crying. She arrived in this country by ship many years ago. The foam sprays off the waves. It returns to the depths as the water breathes it back in.

Alone, Aud hurries back to the fort. A slave, Kolls, hauls wood across the yard. Aud follows him to the forge. He is surprised that she left the funeral.

She reminds Kolls, "Long ago you worked on building one of the ships that bought us here."

He laughs, nervously. "You remember more than I do. I was just a boy back then."

Aud orders him, as the most skilled carpenter alive, to build a ship. It will be a big ship, more than twelve men long, with fifteen pairs of oars. It will carry twenty families, men, women, children, slaves, the best animals, pots, pans, armour, rugs, tapestries, food … everything. And he will build it before spring.

Kolls's mouth drops. How? Problems tumble out of him. "I only build small boats for fishing. It is too cold. We can't bend the wood."

Aud speaks in low tones. "Nobody outside our fort can know we are building the ship. The Picts will attack in winter if they think we will escape. They will kill you too. So we will find a way to work the wood in the cold."

Kolls stares at his feet.

Aud presses on. "When we leave here, when we find a new home – you will not be a slave. Our survival. Your freedom."

Kolls raises his head.

As the cold night winds lift, Aud enters the longhouse. The few returned warriors huddle around the fire. These surviving men debate if they can attack the Picts during winter. Aud listens, knowing there are now too few of them to make war.

In a strong voice, she tells them, "We will cheat the Picts of their revenge. We will sail north in a great ship. We will build it in the forest."

The men are scared. They protest.

"How do we build such a ship?"

"I was not born when you landed on this shore!"

"Who here has navigated by the stars?"

"We will sail north in a great ship. We will build it in the forest."

The warriors roar that they will die by the sword, die with glory!

Aud sighs. "What will the Picts do to our children?"

In the quiet that follows, there is agreement.

And so the ship-building begins. Well before the sun rises, Aud leads the warrior men, the slaves and the strongest of the women deep into the forest.

First, they build a frame, so they can roll their ship to the sea. Kolls calculates that they will need twenty trees. The tallest, straightest trees in the forest are carefully chosen and cut down.

Old people melt down armour and pots to make nails and caulking clamps. Children carry hot pots of barley and vegetables into the forest, to feed the workers.

At night, when the sky is clear, Aud gathers her grandchildren around her. They search out the stars that were first shown to Aud by her father. She shows how the stars make a little bear and there, right at the end of his tail, is the North Star.

This is the star that will lead them to safety. Their ship will sail past the lands of her birth, past the lands of her father to the distant place her brothers travelled to so many years ago. And when the sky is cloudy, their ship will follow the whales as they swim along the currents and the birds as they fly through the air.

The pain in Aud's knees tells her the snow is coming before it falls. The ship-building continues among the snow. As Kolls warned, the bending of the wood is difficult.

In a deep trench, fire boils the water that steams wooden planks. They are bent into shape on pegs that are nailed into a larger wooden board. Only then can each beam be clamped over the previous piece on the ship.

The ship-builders work in the freezing cold, stoking the fires and managing the steaming. This causes the workers' hands to crack and bleed. They rub grease from sheep's wool into their hands to protect their skin.

Piece by piece the ship grows, from the skeleton of a hull to a big bellied vessel.

Soon, the nights get shorter, the days longer. Aud smells the earth opening up. She knows they are running out of time. One morning she wakes to the sounds of birds. Spring is coming.

Aud gives the order. "We must leave now."

Everyone gathers in the gentle rain as six horses pull the ship on its frame out of the forest. The horses stumble across the rocky beach. Aud and Kolls carefully lead the horses to the water. Near the lapping waves, they stop. The horses are released to run off along the beach.

The sea washes around the wooden frame. The ship rises, held up by the water. The builders float their ship into the deeper sea and anchor it. They pack their ship using the smaller fishing boats. Men, women and children run down from the fort to the beach, loading boxes, chickens and pots onto the boats, and then out onto the ship.

Aud walks through the abandoned fort checking that no-one is left behind. There is silence. Aud stands at the entrance, looking out across the land.

Aud notices a thin curl of smoke. The Picts have set up camp. This is the enemy she expected. She hears the shouting of the Pict warriors, the pounding of approaching horses. She doesn't bother to close the gate. She races down to the beach. The slope of the hill helps her. Her old body runs with the spirit of her child self.

Kolls is waiting in the last fishing boat. He stretches out his arms and drags Aud into the little boat. They escape over the foam.

When the fishing boat reaches their magnificent ship, they see the Picts screaming, hollering, cursing at them from the shore. Aud orders the anchor raised.
She stands on the bow as the rhythmic rowing begins. The breeze soon catches their sails, sending them out to sea.

And that is the end of the beginning. Aud guided her people on their long voyage across the North Sea. They finally settled in Iceland where Aud freed Kolls, and all the other slaves, just as she promised.

Noor

*Less than one hundred years ago, in France, during the chaos
and brutality of the Second World War, the gentle and refined
Noor Inayat Khan became a spy …*

Noor's arm feels like it will fall off. She carries a brown leather
suitcase. It is not big, but it is heavy – much heavier than any
normal suitcase. Three of these suitcases would weigh as much
as Noor herself. She is a small woman to be carrying such a
heavy load.

The suitcase handle cuts into Noor's fingers. Her hand is
sweaty too. It is a hot and muggy day. Ahead, she sees soldiers
blocking the road, big men in military uniforms with guns.
Her stomach somersaults. Sandbags form a wall across the
road, so there is only one way through.

She must get past those soldiers, past the checkpoint. She
needs to be unremarkable. This is a challenge. She is a woman
of Indian background, working as a spy for the English in Nazi-
controlled Paris during the Second World War.

Noor lines up behind the others waiting to get through the checkpoint. She puts down her suitcase. She watches soldiers check the people's papers in front of her and look through their bags.

The soldiers take anything that they like the look of. At the front of the line a woman has just lost a packet of sausages.

Noor groans. How will she get through this checkpoint without opening her suitcase? She can't be invisible, so she waves shyly at the soldiers and beckons them to her.

Two soldiers stride over.

Noor whispers, "A man ran away from the checkpoint, down that alley."

Immediately, the soldiers wave her past the other guards, and run off to find the man.

Noor picks up her suitcase, walking past the wall of sandbags and through the checkpoint. She longs to run or at least to turn and see if anyone is following her, but that would look suspicious. So she listens hard to hear if any soldiers are following her.

Half a block further and she turns down a smaller street, out of view of the soldiers.

"Nobody can know I am back in Paris, and my name isn't Noor anymore."

Noor winds her way through the shady back streets of Paris with her heavy suitcase. She avoids the big boulevards.

By the time she reaches her destination her arm is throbbing painfully.

Noor pushes the heavy wooden door. It opens into a courtyard, surrounded by apartments. Washing is strung up across the yard, with a few bicycles and an old pram abandoned against one wall.

Noor lugs her suitcase up the stairs and then knocks on an apartment door. A harried mother with three bouncing children opens up.

The woman hugs Noor. "I didn't know you were back in Paris!"

Noor trills, "Oh look how the children have grown!" Then she whispers "Nobody can know I am back in Paris, and my name isn't Noor anymore. It is Jean-Marie Regnier."

Her friend looks scared. "What are you doing? These are dangerous times."

Noor shakes her head. "I can't tell you, but I really need to go up to the balcony on your roof. Remember the delightful afternoon tea we had up there when we were both studying at university. Can I get up there now?"

On the balcony, Noor looks across the roofs of Paris, feeling the thrill of success. This is perfect. She puts her suitcase down on the ledge between the balcony and the roof. She unlocks it. She opens her suitcase, smiling as if greeting a friend.

Inside is her radio: the transmitter for sending messages, the receiver for getting messages and the power supply. Noor loves the dials, the buttons and copper wire that allow her to communicate with people far, far away.

Happily, she unwinds a long black wire from the case, clambering up and attaching one end to the top of the chimney. This is her aerial.

As a precaution Noor peeks over the balcony railing, looking down to the street. It is almost empty – only one man lugging a cart. All is good.

Noor takes out her Morse code button and positions it on her signals book. This is her special talent.

She doesn't talk through a microphone on her radio, but uses the Morse button to send her messages in a code of dots and dashes. Years of playing the harp and then training in the Air Force have made Noor an especially fast and accurate Morse code operator.

A sound in the distance interrupts Noor. It's a van and it's getting closer. She hears it rumble over the cobblestones below and fear shoots through her. She jumps up, looking for an escape route, but almost immediately Noor realises that the van below is driving quickly, going somewhere else. Not looking for her.

The Nazi enemy is looking for radio operators like Noor. Their vans disguised as bakery trucks or delivery vehicles circle Paris with their own radio technicians inside, trying to pick up other radio signals. But those vans have to drive very slowly. The van below has already passed by.

Relieved, Noor turns her focus back to her message. She taps out that she has found Resistance fighters in Paris ready to receive guns to fight against the Nazis. The radio signals will reach her team in England, and she must wait for their answer.

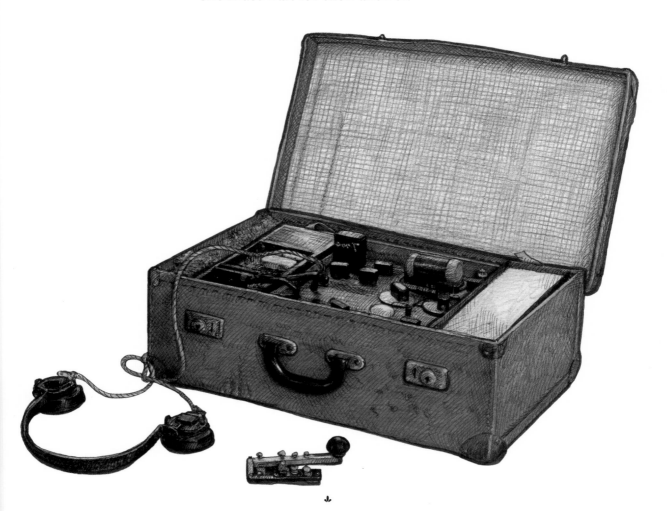

She lies down on the balcony wearing her headphones. She watches the clouds float by in the blue summer sky.

Tap, tap, tap breaks into Noor's daydreaming. It's an incoming message. She marks down the code in her notebook. And then works to decipher it.

"Betrayal. All dead or captured. You are the last radio operator in Paris. DANGER. Come back to London."

Noor trembles. All dead or captured.

She looks back over the balcony, down into the street. No van or trucks.

She looks up to the clouds. "This job has always been dangerous!" she thinks. "I knew that when I started. The Nazis have invaded France. They are violent and cruel, but we can't let them win. I come from brave people. I am a descendant of the great Tipu Sultan and he never surrendered. I am a radio operator. The last radio operator against the Nazis in this city."

Resolutely, Noor types in Morse code. "Staying in Paris. Will continue mission."

She packs away her radio equipment and locks her precious suitcase. Cautiously, she goes down the stairs, thinking hard. "The enemy probably knows who I am and that I am in Paris. I will need to be even more careful."

Her friend is waiting in the stairwell. Noor thanks her as they walk down to the building entrance.

Noor spots the old pram. "Can I take that?" she asks. Her friend nods but looks confused.

Noor laughs. "Everyone wants to know what is in a suitcase. No-one is surprised to see a woman pushing a pram."

Her friend begs Noor to wait and disappears up the stairs. She returns with an armful of food cans, a bag of potatoes and some apples. Together, they hide the suitcase at the bottom of the pram. Noor waves goodbye as she pushes the pram out on to the street.

As the afternoon cools, Noor comes to the next checkpoint. She joins the line. She keeps her head down. The soldier inspects her fake papers and looks into her pram. He is pleased to see food and selects himself a can of peaches before letting Noor go on her way.

Noor survived three months in Paris, sending important information to the English about the French Resistance and the Nazi forces. She was betrayed and finally captured in October 1943. She was imprisoned, interrogated and tortured, but she never revealed a single name of anyone she worked with. After ten months she was executed. Paris was freed of Nazi control in August 1944.

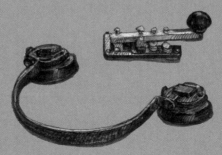

Ping Yang

The Warrior Princess

In China, around 1400 years ago, lived Ping Yang.
She raised an army of thousands before she was
20 years old …

Ping Yang puts on her armour, inspecting her sword before slipping it into her belt. She knows the best sword is not always the hardest sword. The finest swords are flexible, to absorb the shock of each hit. In the same way, the best soldier is not necessarily the strongest.

She slowly breathes in and out to keep calm, control her fear. Today her army will join up with her father's army to attack the walled city of Daxing. Together, they will fight the Emperor's army.

"Not long ago I was a lady of the Imperial Court," remembers Ping Yang. "Now I command my own troops, a fine army that has already won many tough battles."

But Daxing is the heart of the Empire. This battle will decide the war.

Ping Yang mounts her horse. When she was a girl, her father taught her to ride and to hold a sword. But her journey to this moment began when Emperor Yang Di betrayed her father, causing him to rebel. To punish her father for his rebellion, the Emperor imprisoned Ping Yang in Daxing. If it hadn't been for the help of her friend, Ma Sanbao, she would still be in that dungeon.

Ping Yang inspects her 10,000 best soldiers ready for battle. Ma Sanbao rides beside her.

Ping Yang is pleased. "Ma Sanbao, you know the secret of my army?"

"The horses!" he answers.

She shakes her head.

He tries again. "The horse riders. It is near impossible to get good riders."

"No Ma Sanbao. The secret of our army is that we pay our soldiers," Ping Yang explains. "Every other army in the Empire is made up of peasants who must fight for the noble who owns their land. Those poor peasants, forced to go to war with no payment, instead steal from the people they defeat. The peasant armies terrorise the countryside. But our soldiers don't steal. They get paid. That is why the people love us – that is why they join our fight!"

"But it cost you all of your land, your houses and your jewels!" interjects Ma Sanbao.

"What is all that when we are fighting for an empire!" laughs Ping Yang.

She unfurls the banner of the Army of the Lady and charges down the front line of her soldiers, holding the fluttering flag high above her head. The red against the cold blue morning sky. Thousands of soldiers cheer.

Just after sunrise, Ping Yang's father, General Li Yuan, leads his army of thousands to attack the main city gates. The plan is for Ping Yang's father to draw the Emperor's soldiers out of the walled city to fight, then Ping Yang's army will make a surprise strike. Together, General Li Yuan and his daughter will topple the Emperor, take control of the city, and, in doing so, the Empire.

Ping Yang's army of foot soldiers and mounted warriors march towards Daxing. When the massive wall of the city comes into view, Ping Yang cheers. Before them, her father's army battles the Emperor's soldiers. Then her father's forces pretend to retreat, leading the Emperor's army further from the walls of Daxing. Their trap works!

Ping Yang orders her troops to attack close to the city walls, at the rear of the Emperor's army. Her foot soldiers run, yelling into battle. Horses drum the earth. The Emperor's army now fights desperately in two directions. And there is no escape. Ping Yang's army has cut off the possibility of the Emperor's army retreating back into the city.

The harsh noise of battle is crushing: the commotion, the cries, the clash of sword on sword. Ping Yang turns, spotting guards high up on the city walls. Her soldiers are out of range of their arrows. It is then that Ping Yang sees an opportunity to get into the city. In the chaos of battle, she will send soldiers over the city walls!

Ping Yang notices that the ground near the city walls is uneven in colour. She is certain that the darker patches are channels of soft soil that have been dug to trip enemy horses. Such a fall would break the legs of the strongest horse.

Ping Yang hurriedly strategises with Ma Sanbao.

"We could ride around the soft soil?"

"No, it will be too slow – we'll be easy targets for arrows."

"We could send scouts to find the fastest way through the maze of hard and soft ground."

But Ping Yang hates this idea too. "Any soldier riding towards those walls alone will certainly be killed."

Ma Sanbao volunteers to make the ride.

"I command my own troops, a fine army that has already won many tough battles."

"What?" snaps Ping Yang. "No."

Ma Sanbao insists. "I haven't come this far to fail here. We are soldiers." Finally, Ping Yang nods in agreement.

Ma Sanbao rides his horse skilfully between the hard and soft land. He finds a route on firm ground leading to the city walls. From the top of the walls, archers fire zooming arrows. One arrow, like a hawk diving for prey, strikes Ma Sanbao. He falls.

Ping Yang gasps. But there is no time to mourn. Ma Sanbao has shown them the line of attack. She can't waste this moment.

Ping Yang commands the horse riders beside her to charge along the route Ma Sanbao took. Ping Yang's horse thunders across the ground too. Dust rises. Ping Yang keeps her eyes on her target. In front of her, some soldiers fall. The first riders reach the walls. They fling ropes to loop them over the battlements and start to climb.

Drumbeats roll. On top of the walls the city guards are signalling to their soldiers in the field that the city itself is under attack. Ping Yang's climbing soldiers reach the top of the walls as a group of Emperor Yang Di's soldiers turn back towards the city to stop them. But they are too slow. Ping Yang's invading soldiers have succeeded and the huge gates of the city are slowly creaking open.

Ping Yang sees her chance and signals to the soldiers beside her. Together they charge, like a battering ram of horses, soldiers and armour through the Emperor's troops. Ping Yang and her soldiers keep pushing to the city gates and past them.

⚘

They are through the gates! They are inside Daxing! Elated, Ping Yang gallops across the inner courtyard. A small group of her mounted soldiers follow her. She knows this city well and races her horse down its main avenue. This area is usually filled with people, but now everyone hides.

Ping Yang heads straight to the palace. At its steps, she pulls her horse to a halt. Her soldiers stop behind her. The palace is quiet – too quiet. She expects hundreds of soldiers. But there is no-one. Is this a trap?

Cautiously, Ping Yang enters through the magnificent palace doors. As she and her soldiers clank through the palace in their battle armour, servants scurry away from them.

Ping Yang is looking for the Emperor. If she captures the Emperor, the war will be over. The imperial quarters are empty: no wives, no concubines, no servants. And definitely no Emperor.

Ping Yang checks the Grand Hall. Her frustrated cries echo around the empty golden room. She orders her soldiers to open the dungeons and release the prisoners.

Where could the Emperor be hiding? Ping Yang heads to the stables. Only an old mule looks up to greet her. The royal horses are gone. Ping Yang spots a stable worker hiding under a pile of hay. She pulls him out, shouting, "Where is the Emperor?"

"Emperor Yang Di left long ago, long before the battle started," the frightened stable worker cries.

Ping Yang chokes in surprise. "He ran away?"

Ping Yang sends her soldiers out with the news. "Yang Di's gone. He's gone." Like a blast of wind, this fact rips across the battlefields. Soldiers lay down their weapons. The battle is over.

Stained with war, Ping Yang, finally meets her father in the Grand Hall. She collapses in front of the empty throne and weeps. "So many people are dead! Ma Sanbao dead. I will bury him. For what? The Emperor escaped."

Her father implores her to see their victory. "Now that we control the palace and the lands from the north to the south, from the west to the east, where will he go? All Earth is furious at him."

Still Ping Yang sobs. The empty throne room feels like an empty victory.

But it was still a victory. Before long, reports came in that Yang Di had been betrayed and killed by his guards. Ping Yang's father became the new emperor and founder of the Tang Dynasty that ruled China for the next three hundred years. Ping Yang was honoured as a princess and a general.

Te Puea

THE HEALING PRINCESS

·

More than 100 years ago, Te Puea cared for her people, the Māori
people of Waikato, as they suffered the consequences of the English
colonists stealing their land …

Te Puea walks along the riverbank early in the morning.
The mud feels good, squishing between her toes. Her
quiet moment is disturbed when she sees a man bent over,
crouching at the water. She moves closer. He is groaning,
rocking back and forth. He is a big man, about thirty years old,
but he looks like a distressed child.

Gently, she touches his shoulder. "What's wrong?"

He turns his face to look at her. He is one of her people.
She knows him but struggles to recognise him. His face
is covered with sores. Some of the sores look like peas
stuck under his skin. Some sores are open and liquid oozes
from them.

He cries, "I'm burning. My mouth is burning."

Te Puea reels back in shock, but recovers herself quickly. This man needs her help. Her deep voice soothes him as she guides him to his feet. Gently, she leads him up towards the settlement. She sits the man on a bench in the community meeting hall. He lies down, unable to support his own weight.

She comforts him then reassures him, "I'll be right back."

Dashing to her home, Te Puea calls out to her sister, Hera. "Water, I need water."

Te Puea doesn't go inside her house. Instead she waits for Hera to come out. Her shouting alerts some of the old people and children who live in the settlement. They all come to see what the problem is.

Te Puea orders them, "Stay back – don't come close to me."

Te Puea returns to the sick man with water. Only Hera follows her. Te Puea lays down a mat for him on the floor, making a comfortable bed. She motions to her sister, and the two of them move the man to the mat so he can rest. They give him water.

He drinks desperately, as though he has been lost in the desert. Then he collapses into sleep.

Te Puea goes outside, takes off her sack cloth apron and throws it on the fire. Then she washes her hands and face in the outdoor bucket. She orders Hera to do the same. This scares and confuses Hera.

Tu Puea accepts it is her responsibility to look after her people.

But Te Puea talks calmly to her, and to everyone who has gathered around outside.

No-one can remember an illness like this.

One of the old women suggests, "Maybe it is a terrible case of chickenpox."

Others grumble that it is sorcery, makutu, making the poor man sick.

Te Puea hushes this worried talk. She promises that whatever has caused his suffering, they will look after the man. Then she tells the crowd that she doesn't want anyone else near him except her or her sister.

Te Puea makes her patient a nutritious fish soup using the catch from the river. She keeps boiling water too, so that he has plenty to drink. She and Hera take turns fanning the man and covering him in wet cloths when he burns with fever. Te Puea sings, so that he knows he is not alone.

The next morning a young man and woman knock on Te Puea's door. They are shaking. Lots of small bumps cover their faces, it looks like rice is trapped under their skin. Te Puea puts her hand on the woman's forehead. She is hot, and sweat is making her skin clammy.

Soon, more sick people come. Te Puea is not surprised. She is the grand-daughter of King Tawhiao, and Te Puea accepts it is her responsibility to look after her people.

There are stories of men and women dying up and down the river. This is a terrible disease.

An emergency meeting to discuss the disease is organised by Te Puea with the elders and her family. There is one question everyone wants the answer to. Where has this come from? People bring rumours that it is a Pakeha disease, a disease that the Europeans have bought them. This makes sense to Te Puea. The anger of the gods has not caused this suffering, but instead an illness bought by Europeans to her Māori community.

Te Puea thinks of asking the Europeans for a cure to this European disease, but at this time most hospitals won't allow Māori people in them. In Waikato, Te Puea's whole district, there is only one hospital in the city of

Hamilton that will admit Māori people. When Te Puea asks her people, no-one wants to go there. The hospital is far away and no-one trusts the Pakeha to care for them.

There is only one solution. Te Puea sends out the message – everyone who is sick in the lower river settlements must come to her. They need to get the sick to a safe place, away from their families so they don't spread the disease.

The message travels fast and so the sick people come. Te Puea has no hospital, but she will make do. She orders the building of open-air shelters thatched with nikau palms.

Te Puea organises Hera and other women to nurse the sick in shifts, but Te Puea herself works day and night.

One day, as Te Puea feeds a patient, Hera comes running to her, "There is a Pakeha man here and he says he is closing us."

This makes no sense to Te Puea, so she asks Hera to care for the patient while she goes to find out what the Pakeha man means.

A man in uniform is waiting for her by the gate.

"You are quarantined," he announces. "Nobody can leave this settlement until there is government permission to do so. This is a small pox outbreak and we can't have you Māoris tracking it all over the country."

Te Puea wants to shout at him. "Small pox! Māoris tracking it all over the country! You bought it to us!" Instead she asks, "So who will bring us the flour, sugar, tea and butter that we usually buy?"

The man shrugs.

Te Puea presses on. "What about medical supplies? We need help with the fever."

The man shakes his head. Te Puea turns her back on the man. She has nothing else to say to him. She returns to her patients and her sister.

Hera is full of questions.

Te Puea gives her the important details. "This disease is a Pakeha disease. Our people have small pox. We can't leave the settlement, they won't help us at all and we can't go shopping for supplies."

Hera gestures to the shelters that house their patients. "How will we feed everyone?"

Te Puea answers with confidence. "The river. Fish and eel, and we'll catch pigeons."

Hera grins. "Well, we have a bit of work to do then."

Te Puea smiles, and the two women return to caring for their sick.

For more than a month Te Puea worked at incredible speed, looking after the ill. Astonishingly, no-one in her care died during the 1913 small pox epidemic. However this was not the last epidemic that Te Puea had to fight. In 1918, her community was struck by a terrible flu. Te Puea herself got very sick, but she survived to establish and run community care for the many orphans the flu left behind.

Nzinga

THE MIGHTY PRINCESS

In the Kingdom of Ndongo, around 400 years ago, Nzinga confronted the Portuguese colonialists who stole her people …

Nzinga commands, "Bring me the axe."

A servant scurries out of the building, quickly returning with a small but sharp axe. He bows as he hands the weapon to Nzinga. She ties the axe to her belt, using the leather cord attached to the painted handle.

Nzinga's younger sister, Mukambu, silently watches this, feeling hot with anxiety even though it is cool inside the large room with its thick mud walls and the high thatched ceiling.

Finally, Mukambu can keep quiet no longer. "I thought you were going to talk. Why do you need the axe if you are just talking? Why do you need the axe to negotiate a treaty? What are you planning sister?"

Nzinga laughs. "To get anything from these murderers – we need to look just as murderous." She drops her smile. "We have

to win back some of the thousands of our people who have been kidnapped and taken as slaves by the Portuguese."

Mukambu looks at the ground. "But the axe is our brother's. He is king. He is still king. You can't wear it."

Nzinga shakes her head. "He is a king hiding on the Kindonga Islands."

"He's not hiding. He's a prisoner!"

Nzinga ignores her sister's comment. "There is no king here to negotiate with these thieves, to save our people. Our brother can't do this, so I must. This new Portuguese governor must know that I speak for the power of Ndongo. We are the power of Ndongo. I will also wear our brother's robe." Nzinga points at the door and the servant rushes off to collect the robe.

Nzinga is carried to the governor's fort by servants, who hold her chair above their shoulders. Wrapped in the king's robe, carrying the ceremonial axe, Nzinga rides high above all else. The courtiers clear the path of common people before her as they trek up the hill. Nzinga's sisters and servants trail behind her. The transport of Nzinga is a glorious procession. She looks out across the rich green of her country. This is her land.

But the Portuguese have stolen so many of her people that they can no longer farm this land and many of her people are starving. For her whole life, her country has been attacked by the Portuguese. When she was a child, her father insisted she learn Portuguese, and he also taught her about negotiation and war.

The procession reaches the gates of the Portuguese fortress, but Nzinga does not dismount. Her servants carry her deep into the heart of the building.

The Portuguese soldiers, with shiny helmets and long staffs, run before Nzinga's procession, leading the way to the governor.

The governor sits on a chair carved from dark wood in a large white room. When Nzinga is carried in, he does not stand to show respect. He just twirls his moustache. Behind him, his guards stand in a row. Nzinga's servants gently lower her to the ground.

She stands tall. Nzinga immediately spots the insult. The governor has provided no chair for her. There is nowhere for her to sit.

She fumes, thinking, "Does he expect me to stand before him as if he is a prince?"

No-one speaks, but the governor smirks. With a wave of his hand he motions to a mat on the floor, as if Nzinga will sit before him like a peasant.

Nzinga wants to throw her brother's axe at the governor, but she controls her anger. She will not be humbled by this insult. She will not sit on that mat.

Her eyes dart around the room. It is bare.

The chair she was carried up on has no legs and is woven from straw. It will not do. There is nothing else in this room except her servants and followers. Nzinga motions to one of her servants. She orders the man to kneel on the mat, then put down his hands so that he becomes a bench. Nzinga regally sits on top of her crouching servant.

The governor is flabbergasted. Nzinga places the axe gently on her lap. She looks straight into the eyes of the governor.

He shifts awkwardly in his seat and angrily asserts, "The old king, your father, allowed us to trade. But now your people kill my soldiers and block the roads!"

"Your soldiers do not trade. Your soldiers steal my people. Men, women, children. Families. Whole villages," corrects Nzinga. "Everyone in the valley.

⚘

And the next valley and the valley after that. Across the plains. Deep in the jungle. We cannot count all the people you have stolen in the last three dry seasons. You steal our peasants. So many of them that we can't farm our lands. You load boat after boat with more and more people. You pay our neighbours, the Imbangala, to attack us. So we lose more of our people to a war that you started. You cut the body of Ndongo and drain our blood. "So, yes, we attack your soldiers. We will drain your blood. We will drain as much blood from you as we can." Nzinga holds up her ceremonial axe and catches the light from the window on its sharp blade. She admires the weapon. "Unless you give us a reason to stop."

The governor remembers the many dead Portuguese soldiers. He has read about the rebellion under the last governor. He knows Nzinga's people can wage war.

So he asks, "What do you need to stop?"

Nzinga is ready. "You Portuguese want to trade and

"There is no king ... to save our people. Our brother can't do this, so I must."

take lots of slaves. We will let you trade in the harbours. We will help you on the slave routes, but we have three demands. If you meet these demands you will have peace. Peace will make you rich."

Nzinga sits up a little taller on her servant's back. "Firstly, the peasants that you have not yet sent away must be returned to us – those you are holding prisoner in the harbour. All of them. You can get your bodies from the north or the east, but not from Ndongo. "Secondly, stop paying the Imbangala to attack us.

"Thirdly, your soldiers must leave the fort on the Lucala River."

Nzinga gazes unblinkingly at the governor before continuing. "If you do not do these three things, I will order all people in Ndongo to make war with you all day, every day."

The governor pulls again at his moustache. He makes excuses why he can't meet Nzinga's terms.

He has already sold the peasants, he lies saying that he doesn't pay the Imbangala to make war, and he claims he is not allowed to evacuate the fort on the Lucala River.

Nzinga smiles and lifts her axe. "Then it is war."

The governor stumbles over his words, trying to take back what he has said. He doesn't want war. War is expensive. The governor agrees to negotiate.
There are hours of discussion about trade routes, tributes of slaves, the protection of Portuguese priests and numbers of soldiers. It is a fierce battle of words, but

finally the exhausted governor agrees that he will sign a treaty with Nzinga.

Now Nzinga stands. Her servant groans. As she leaves she turns back to the governor. She smiles at him. "Governor, maybe as a gift, you should keep my servant. You clearly need more furniture." With that she sweeps out of the room.

Shortly after this famous encounter Nzinga became queen. The Portuguese broke their promises to her, so she led her people in war against them. She won and lost battles, inspired stories of her bravery and brutality. She was Queen of Ndongo for a long, long time, until her death at 82 years of age.

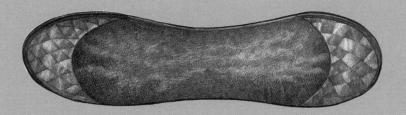

Alice

THE ARTFUL PRINCESS

More than one hundred years ago, Alice was born profoundly deaf but learnt to lip-read and speak English, German, French and Greek. During the Second World War, in Athens, she hid and protected a Jewish family in her house …

Alice feels the floor vibrate as soldiers bang on her front door.

Her servant trembles, silently mouthing the words, "It is the Gestapo."

Alice nods, tucking her greying hair behind her ears.

The servant barely breathes, "What about upstairs? If the Gestapo find the family they will kill them … and kill us too."

On the top storey of the very same building another woman, Rachael, hears the banging. She signals for silence. Her adult daughter, Tilda, lays down her book. Her son, Michel, puts down his pen. The three of them listen carefully to what is happening downstairs.

The hammering at the front door gets stronger. Alice touches the cross on her necklace and murmurs a prayer to quiet her fear, then she orders her servant, "After I open the front door, go shopping. Leave calmly."

The servant mouthes, "What about you?"

Alice raises an eyebrow. "I will fight them with the best weapon I have: good manners."

With that Alice, in her plain house-coat, walks into the entrance hall. With one fast movement, she swings the front door open. In stumbles the soldier who had been pounding the door.

Alice smiles. "Good afternoon, gentlemen."

The commandant in full uniform does the "heil Hitler" salute. Six soldiers push into the house.

The commandant announces in German. "We are here to search this house."

Alice, half his height, sweetly shakes her head. She answers in perfect German, "What are you saying? I can't hear you. I am deaf." She points at her ear.

"We are here to search your house, Princess," the commandant booms.

Alice waves away his irritation. "Don't all stand around in the entrance hall. We can't talk here. Please, come into the sitting room. Make yourself comfortable."

Upstairs, Rachael kneels on the wooden floorboards, pressing her ear to the floor. She can hear men's voices. Rachael whispers, "Tilda and Michel, hide anything that shows we are here."

They pack away books, reading glasses, note paper and the sewing basket, moving with special care to not drop anything or make a floorboard creak.

This time the commandant uses Alice's official title when he addresses her. "Princess Andrew, we are here to search your home!"

The princess squints at him. "Princess Andrew. Funny. Nobody has addressed me by my husband's name for quite a while."

"No, Princess – we will search your house!" the commandant yells again.

Alice answers quietly, "Prince George."

"What?" splutters the confused commandant.

"This is the house of my brother-in-law, Prince George," explains Alice.

The commandant groans, before yelling again, "We are here to search your home!"

"Oh, you've come about the house!" Alice thanks them. "The whole place is falling down. It is this terrible war. There's nobody to fix anything now. To the kitchen!"

She bustles off down the hallway. "We used to have running water, but listen to the pipe when I turn it on."

No water comes out.

The princess grabs a soup ladle, hitting the pipe over and over again. The soldiers flinch at the sharp, clanging sound.

Upstairs, Rachael heeds the echoing warning signal. It's time to go into their hiding spot.

The princess continues banging the pipe. "See, no water comes out. Get one of your boys under there and find out what is going on."

The commandant yells again. "You didn't hear me – we will search the house! Search the house!"

Rachael and Michel move the wardrobe away from the wall. There is small hole leading into the roof space. Tilda climbs in first. Rachael follows. Michel is last. He reaches out, grabs the side of the wardrobe, jerking it back towards the wall. The old wardrobe scrapes across the floor.

Downstairs, a soldier hears the wardrobe moving. He asks Alice what that sound was.

Alice continues banging the pipe. "You need to fix things! I am the great-granddaughter of Queen Victoria and I have no running water!"

The commandant seethes with frustration.

The soldiers search the kitchen, opening cupboards and looking through her food. "There is a lot of food here for one woman."

Alice shuts the cupboard door. "I feed the poor."

Like a mother duck, the princess shoo-shoos all the soldiers out of her kitchen and into the dining room.

The soldiers check under rugs and along the walls for hidden doors. During this search, Alice explains the history of the paintings on the walls.

When the soldiers

want to leave the room, she continues talking about the paintings but turns her back on the soldiers, blocking the doorway so she cannot see their protests or read their lips.

Finally, Alice finishes her description of the last artwork and cheerfully leads the men into the hallway.

Rachael, Tilda and Michel crouch in the tiny dark space. They listen to their own breathing and strain to hear sounds in the house. It is warm with the three of them so close together. Rachael runs her hand over Tilda's hair.

In the downstairs hallway, Alice continues her art lecture.

The commandant interrupts the princess. "A man was seen entering your home."

The princess pretends not to hear or understand as she points out a photo hanging on the wall. "These are my daughters. Aren't they handsome women?"

The commandant repeats himself. "Can you hear me? A suspicious man was seen entering your home. He never left."

Alice rattles on. "Of course, all my girls married German princes." Alice tells them about each prince and his current rank in the German army, and Nazi Party.

"I will fight them with the best weapon I have: good manners."

When she pauses for breath, the commandant repeats tiredly, "A man in your home?"

Alice claps her hands and directs the soldiers upstairs. Now she will show them the impressive collection of paintings by Prince Nicholas. The soldiers behind her groan.

In the roof, Rachael, Tilda and Michel feel each thud, thud, thud – boots on the stairs as the soldiers get closer.

Upstairs, Alice complains of the peeling wallpaper, the broken heating and the rattling windows. She explains the history of every painting, vase and statue. The bored soldiers now barely pretend to search the rooms. The shadows grow longer as the day gets darker. Still, Alice chatters away.

The impatient commandant orders an immediate search of the top floor. Alice tells him not to interrupt her story. Her aunt was killed by the Bolsheviks in Russia. They should all show respect. When Alice finally finishes, she ushers them up the stairs to the top level.

Now Rachael, Tilda and Michel hear every word that is said.

"Here I have a big trunk full of photos of my family." Alice promises, "I will show each and every one, all the royals of Europe! So many stories!"

The soldiers mutter complaints.

Rachael hears the commandant on the landing:

❧

"We can't stay to look at more photos or paintings. We apologise, Princess Andrew, but we must return to the offices. The house has cleared the inspection." Rachael breathes deeper as the boots clump, clump, clump down the stairs.

Alice closes the front door behind the soldiers. She holds her cross and thanks God that they have left.

In the dark Alice goes back up the stairs and pushes out the wardrobe. Rachael, Tilda and Michel crawl out.

Rachael apologises. "You would have been killed, Princess, if they knew."

Alice waves her hand dismissively. "They are hunting your people, hunting you. What did you expect me to do? Did your husband not save the king of Greece? We owe your family."

She takes Rachael's hand. "But we need to be very, very careful from now on. Their spies must have seen Michel come to the house. We are being watched."

Rachael smiles. "Yes, but I don't think those men will rush back in a hurry."

Alice laughs.

Rachael, Tilda and Michel survived the war, living in the top of Alice's home until Athens was freed by the Allied forces in 1944. After the war, Alice founded an order of nuns, gave away all of her possessions and dedicated her life to helping the poor.

Clotilda

THE REBEL PRINCESS

*In the Frankish kingdoms, almost 1400 years ago, lived Clotilda,
a young princess sent to a convent after the death of
the king, her father ...*

Clotilda, comfortable on her horse, gazes up at the walls of the
convent. What a fortress! Only the cross above the gates shows
that this is a house of religion.

The guards surrounding her sigh in relief. After days on
dangerous roads, they have delivered the princess safely.
Clotilda doesn't share their happiness.

The travellers' horses clatter through the gates into the convent's
inner courtyard. Nuns stand in lines to welcome Princess
Clotilda. Their robes are the colour of dry dirt. Clotilda knows
that her cousin, another princess who is the same age as her,
lives here but none of these women look like princesses.

One woman does stand out, an older woman who is clearly
in charge – the Abbess. Her cloak is rich black, lined with fur.
Hanging from her belt is a long thin rod.

She commands the guards of the travelling party to retire for food and drink. They gratefully agree, leaving Clotilda without a backward glance.

Clotilda is led along the convent's covered walkways to the Abbess's own rooms. There, Clotilda is stripped of her regal garments.

"I, too, need to eat and drink," complains Clotilda.

The Abbess flicks her bare legs with the cane.

Clotilda protests. "I am Clotilda," she shouts, "daughter of the king of Paris!"

The Abbess growls, "He is dead. You're 17 years old and you've refused to marry – so now you will obey me!"

She throws Clotilda some brown robes.

Clotilda hates everything here. The itchy clothing, the watery soup and the straw that is to be her new bed.

While the nuns prepare for slumber, lonely Clotilda listens to the distant music of a lute played down in the Abbess's rooms. Finally sleep finds her.

BONG, BONG, BONG!

Clotilda wakes, confused. It is dark. A young nun whispers to her, "The bells! Quickly, we must go to the chapel for Lauds."

Clotilda struggles to her feet. The nuns shuffle into the chapel, Clotilda among them. The warmth of one candle greets them.

"Nuns don't promise to starve! We didn't choose to come here."

As they kneel for their prayers, the young nun turns to Clotilda, and in a whisper reveals herself. "I am your cousin, Basina."

As the days pass, Basina helps Clotilda adjust to life in the convent. She shows Clotilda the sharpest shears for garden work, teaches her the easiest way to carry water and how to milk goats without getting kicked.

In the walled garden, Clotilda sees the laden fruit trees and vegetable gardens with fat chickens roaming about.

It makes her angry. "With so much, why are we always hungry?" she demands.

Basina struggles to explain. "Nuns promise obedience and poverty."

Clotilda snorts. "Nuns don't promise to starve!" she says. "We didn't choose to come here. You are Princess Basina – you are the daughter of a king!"

Basina laughs at her cousin. "He has been dead much longer than your father."

Clotilda snaps back. "Yes, killed by your step-mother!"

"Quiet dear cousin," warns Basina, "if you keep on like this you will get a beating, get locked in the cellar, or worse."

Basina is right. Before long Clotilda gets a solid thrashing. It is Palm Sunday. Most of the work in the convent stops for prayer that day, but the animals still have to be cared for. Clotilda milks a goat, then she lifts the bucket to her lips and drinks. The Abbess flies like a bat across the yard, her cane uplifted. She slashes it down on Clotilda. Again and again. And with every blow, Clotilda's fury grows.

That night, the nuns file into the dimly lit dining hall. Candles flicker in tall stands by the walls.

Clotilda raises her nose and sniffs. "Oh, I am looking forward to dinner tonight," she says. "I smell fish cooking, roasting vegetables ..."

Basina motions for her to be quiet. "That's for the Abbess," she whispers.

Another girl in line complains, "We never eat fish or meat. I'm hungry."

Other nuns inhale as if they can feed on the smells.

Clotilda whispers, just loud enough for all to hear, "The Abbess eats what she wishes, when she wishes, ignoring the wishes of God. She entertains men. She drinks our wine. She steals our food. So why does she rule over us?"

The women sit down at long tables. Bowls of weak soup are placed before them. The old cook puts an empty bowl in front of Clotilda.

"What?" Clotilda shouts.

The cook stammers, "Abbess says you've eaten your share. The goat milk."

Clotilda stands and hurls her empty bowl across the dining hall. "We are hungry!" she shouts. Clotilda bangs the table. The cook flees. Nuns start to bang their bowls on the table.

Basina sitting next to Clotilda groans. Clotilda starts chanting to the rhythm of the banging bowls.

"We are hungry! We are hungry!"
The women roar together. "We are hungry!"

The Abbess rushes into the dining hall, flanked by male guards. She waves her rod menacingly.

The guards dash forward with sticks. They beat the women and girls, hurling them to the floor. Some nuns throw bowls at the attackers. Others throw fists. Basina shields a younger nun from blows by the guards.

"You eat our food!" some of the women cry. "Abbess, you drink wine with men! You steal from the convent!"

Amid the chaos, bowls are knocked off tables. Lit candles fall to the floor.

Clotilda yells to the nuns. "Fire! Get out! Run!"

Following Clotilda, the nuns push their way out of the dining hall and tear along the walkways. Crossing the courtyard, Clotilda laughs and leads the charge to the gates.

Basina, finding her voice, shouts, "To St. Hilda's church in town!"

Clotilda and Basina grin at each other, and the crowd of women race down from the convent into the streets of the town below.

In the dark of St. Hilda's church, Clotilda starts to plan. "We need to take the convent. It is well fortified and has food."

Basina agrees. "We have to do whatever is necessary to protect the women and girls." The nuns cheer.

Clotilda frowns. "We'll need an army."

"No. We don't. A mob will do," answers Basina. She points across the town square to the candle-lit tavern.

Clotilda pulls the tavern door open. The sight of her stills the voices of everyone inside. Men look up from their meals. Most have impressive scars.

Clotilda promises the men gold and free food if they fight for her. Some return to their dinner, but enough of them gather their work tools as weapons and follow Clotilda.

In the dark of night, Clotilda leads the nuns and the mob back up the hill to the convent. The air seems fresher, the cold bracing. They creep forward.

"How will we smash through the gates?" Basina whispers.

"No smashing," chuckles Clotilda. "You will knock on the door and beg forgiveness, and when the guard opens the gates we will storm in."

The plan works. As the gates open a crack, the tavern men push through.

Fighting ignites in the convent courtyard. Yelling, punching, kicking. The convent guards are outnumbered.

Screams ring out from the dormitory. Clotilda is running up as angry nuns throw the Abbess down the stairs. Clotilda catches her. The Abbess's hair is wild, her face panicked. Clotilda orders the nuns to stop beating the

Abbess, and instead to lock her in the cellar.

Clotilda and Basina, separated in the chaos, meet again in the convent's covered walkways. They hug. They've done it! They have taken over the convent. All around them the sounds of smashing furniture and yelling echo.

Basina whispers, "Now you have to get this under control."

"Food," answers Clotilda, firmly. "It is time we all had that promised dinner."

Just before dawn, the convent is quiet once more.

The well-fed nuns are asleep in their dormitory. The men, also with full bellies, sleep in the convent's covered walkways.

Still awake, Clotilda and Basina inspect the damage and double check the gates are locked. They have secured the convent, but Clotilda knows that this rebellion will anger this land's powerful men.

And Clotilda was right. The Count of Poitou attacked the convent, trying to make the women surrender. He failed. The bishops ex-communicated Clotilda and Basina, throwing them out of the Church, but still the women did not surrender. Finally their cousin, the new king, negotiated with them. Basina chose to stay at the convent as a nun, making peace with the Abbess. Clotilda was given back her lands. She ruled them until her death. She never married.

Asmau

THE WISE PRINCESS

*In the Sokoto Caliphate around 200 years ago, lived Nana
Asmau, a great poet, scholar and teacher in four languages:
Fulfulde, Hausa, Tuareg and Arabic …*

Nana Asmau folds the manuscript and slips it into its leather
pouch. She takes the pouch, puts it in another satchel and
hangs the satchel on her bedroom wall.

There are hundreds of satchels hanging on the wall – each one
protecting manuscripts from the dry sands of the Sahara. This
is Asmau's library. In the middle of the circular room stands a
raised bed covered with clean white sand.

There are no luxuries, other than the manuscripts, that show
this woman is the daughter of the founder of the Caliphate,
sister to the Caliph and wife to the Caliph's most important
advisor. Asmau is known for her simple life.

Her reading time is disturbed by an excited little girl at her
door.

"They are coming, they are coming!" the girl calls. Asmau smiles and follows the bouncing child out to the sunny courtyard.

It is joyful when the students come. Each group is a chorus of laughter and fun; a combination of girls under 14 and older women who no longer have children to raise.

Organising and caring for the students is a head teacher, called the jaji. She stands out in the group because the jaji always wears a black hat. The jaji knows what should be learnt, she chooses the students and she leads them across the sometimes dangerous country to Nana Asmau's home.

For village women, the journey into the bustling town of Sokoto is exciting. When Asmau set up this education system, she had no idea the happiness it would create.

But on this morning, even before Asmau sees the procession, she knows something is wrong. She hears the singing of the choral group. Their song is sad and slow.

The singers are the first to walk through the family gates. Next, comes a donkey with a small girl on its back. She doesn't wave or smile.

The other students follow with their heads down. Asmau recognises faces, but someone is missing. No woman wears the black hat of the jaji.

When Asmau set up this education system, she had no idea the happiness it would create.

🌱

Asmau rushes forward looking concerned. "Where is your jaji? Where is Hauwa?"

One of the young girls pipes up. "Hauwa died."
An older woman passes Asmau the black hat.

Holding the hat, Asmau closes her eyes and prays, "May Allah have mercy on her and reward her for her good works."

Asmau then shepherds the sad women and girls into her home. There is a large meal waiting for the students. The conversations are quiet and thoughtful. The girls tell Asmau about Hauwa's quiet death from old age.

Asmau remembers her friend. "She was an excellent teacher, an excellent jaji. She was always on the road bringing new students to me during the dry season, the wet season, the harvest, the time of dust storms and the start of the rains."

Asmau asks the women how the procession travelled safely to Sokoto without their jaji. The women assure her that they had no problems. Everyone across the lands recognises that they are students of Asmau and wouldn't challenge her authority by attacking them – even without their jaji.

After the meal, the women and girls offer Asmau the gifts from their village – honey, grain, cloth, butter and thread. Asmau gratefully accepts it all, understanding how much harder it must have been to organise these gifts while they mourned their jaji. She sends the gifts to be shared among the sick and orphaned of Sokoto.

Over the next days, Asmau instructs the women how to wash properly before prayer, what a Muslim woman should wear and what prayers they should learn. She hears about the quarrels from the village and listens as the women tell her about the health problems of their families.

They study both law and medicine. Together, the women plan solutions to all sorts of daily problems. Through all this is the beautiful chanting of the younger girls memorising poems and parts of the Qur'an.

These are very busy days, and Asmau misses the support of the jaji.

Looking at the women before her, Asmau asks herself: "Who here has the strength, intelligence and religious understanding to be the head teacher for all these women and girls? Is it the always smiling Habiba, the pious Aisha, or the sensible Amina?"

Practical concerns run through her mind. These women are now all too old to have children, but are any of these women still responsible for young children or the elderly or the sick?

To be the jaji requires time not only to teach, but also to help people solve their problems, to heal the ill, to resolve conflicts and to travel great distances with the new students.

In the evenings, Asmau retires to her poetry and writing in her mother language. She also helps her husband with the complex administration of the Caliphate, reading in Arabic about trade and taxation and raids from the Gobir army. But once everyone else is asleep she paces, thinking and grieving for the loss of a wise teacher.

Finally, one morning after prayer, Asmau decides that smiling Habiba is reliable, strong and will bring joy to teaching. "Habiba will be the new jaji if she wants the job."

When Asmau asks her, Habiba's smile covers half her face.

On the last morning, everyone gathers in the courtyard. Asmau congratulates them all on the days of intensive learning, even while they were still grieving for Hauwa.

"Knowledge is the precious gift that we share and pass on to others. Knowledge is as the great Niger River, providing water for all Hausa-land, its waters spreading out in all directions. And in the same way, all you do will be graced by your learning. And your new jaji to guide you on your journey will be the joyful and wise Habiba." Habiba steps forward and kneels.

Asmau places the black woven malfa hat on Habiba's head.

Next, Asmau ties a strip of red cloth around the brim of the hat. "And this cloth is the symbol of my authority. As you travel the land, all will know that you have my protection. Bless you, Habiba – you are now a jaji."

Asmau watches the procession pass out of her family gates with the black hat of the new jaji in the middle of the group. She listens. Their now joyful singing gets fainter and fainter as they walk away, on their journey home.

For the rest of Nana Asmau's life she continued the expansion of her education system. She died at the age of 71, but her network of jajis and learned women continued to thrive and grow for another forty years until the invasion of the British in 1903. Today, more than sixty of her writings survive, including works of poetry, history and eulogies for those she loved and respected.

✦

Lozen

THE SAGE PRINCESS

In Apache, more than 100 years ago, Lozen was a warrior, a prophetess and a medicine woman of the Chihenne Chiricahua Apache. She fought in the Apache Wars …

Lozen squeezes Ela's hand. Ela shudders with pain.

Once the pain passes, Lozen rises, walking away from the pregnant woman. Lozen approaches the chief, her brother Victorio, who is waiting with the warriors.

Lozen looks down, respectfully, as she speaks. "Ela vomited. It is a sign her baby is coming. Soon. Very soon. Ela cannot travel any further. We are fighting for survival. Survival means our children. I have to help bring her child into the world."

Victorio looks down at the ground also. "I am sorry, sister, that we can't wait with you. We have to keep going and cross the border."

Victorio's face is lined by a lifetime of struggle. "We will miss you. How will we know where the Mexican and American soldiers are without your insight from the Goddess, the White Painted Woman? But you are right, younger sister, if we leave Ela, she will die and her child too. That is certain. Everything else is uncertain. So you must stay."

Victorio orders the other warriors to mount their horses.

"You have to take our horses," Lozen interrupts. "We can't have the animals giving away our location to the armies tracking us."

Victorio nods. He has no fear taking Lozen's horse. Lozen's name means "horse thief". He knows she will find a horse when she needs a horse. Nobody can charm horses like she can.

Victorio and the warriors gallop off, along the ridge. Lozen and Ela are left alone with a gun, a blanket tied by rope, a small bag of food, a bottle of water and Lozen's knife.

The women are high above the desert. The ground is rocky and spare. Where can they hide? They need a safe place. Lozen sees a lone tree, crooked like an old woman – so bent over that she almost touches the earth.

Around the tree is long dry grass. Together, Lozen and Ela stagger over. Lozen clears the rocks and lays a blanket close to the base of the tree. She then adjusts the grass, so there is no evidence that they have walked through it.

"Ela, you are going to be a mother again before the sun goes down."

In the shade of the tree Lozen listens at Ela's huge belly to the heart beats.

"Your heart beat is strong like the pounding of horses hooves. Your baby's heart races like a rabbit. Two different rhythms making perfect music. We will do this."

But Ela is worried. "Many women don't make it through this journey."

Lozen nods and smiles. "You are young. You are strong. Thank the heavens this is not your first child. You know what you are doing."

Ela grimaces in pain. It passes.

Lozen opens up her pouch. She pulls out a gnarled root and whittles off the bark with her knife. She gives Ela the soft yellow core to chew on. "It will help dull the pain."

Then Lozen throws the rope over the thickest tree branch. "You will grasp each end of the rope. The tree will hold you up so you can push down."

Ela smiles.

Night rises around them. With the darkness comes desert cold. Lozen leans against the tree and her friend leans against her.

Lozen wraps her arms around Ela. She feels her contractions. Lozen counts her pulse beats for each rush of pain and the peace between. The moments of pressure come faster as they should for Ela.

The dark before dawn brings real cold. Lozen preserves their water by drinking the dew on the leaves.
With the rising sun, Lozen senses their enemies are close. There are many of them.

Lozen creeps out from the shelter of the tree and runs up the ridge between the rocks. From the top of the ridge she looks down either side. She sighs. Through the valley to her west she sees United States Cavalry.

Leading these soldiers are trackers, but she doesn't panic. They are looking for Apache warriors on horseback, not two women hiding among the rocks.
To the east, she sees a smaller band of Mexican soldiers.

Like a cat, Lozen creeps back through the grass to her friend. She whispers, "We are surrounded. You have to bring this baby into the world silently."

Lozen rips a gag from the end of her shirt and gives it to Ela to bite down on.

Ela holds on to the two ends of the rope, bites down on the gag and pushes. The waves of pressure come faster and faster. There is no peace between them now. Ela's whole body works.

Lozen whispers, "I see the top of your child's head. There is not too much blood. Ela, you are going to be a mother again before the sun goes down."

Lozen wipes the sweat from her friend's forehead, but it still courses down her neck and chest. Ela's face is red with effort and heat. Her face contorts as she bites down on the gag. She makes almost no sound.

Both women hear horses and men's voices. Lozen peeks through the grass, watching soldiers pass close by, one after another. They are a scouting party looking out across the desert, not at the rocks or tree nearby. Unsuspecting, the men ride down the hill.

Silently, tears run from Ela's eyes. Her nose runs. Sweat drips from her. Lozen pours some of their precious water over Ela's face. She sucks the now wet rag. Still, she clings to the rope from the tree.

And, as Lozen promised, the baby comes, curled up like a blue bud. As the baby stretches out, he cries.

Lozen thanks the creator god, Ussen, that the soldiers are not passing by now. She helps Ela lie back on the blanket and places the little boy straight onto his mother's chest. The baby knocks his head on Ela as he crawls for his mother's breast. Seeing the baby's strength, Lozen cries joyfully.

Lozen reaches in her pouch, mixing bark from a plant branch with water for Ela to drink. It ensures that Ela will not continue to bleed.

Lozen waits until the umbilical cord has stopped pulsing. Now Lozen digs a small hole in the dirt, laying dry grass at the bottom and lights a fire using her two flint rocks. The fire burns fast and hot. There is little smoke for the enemy soldiers to spot. Lozen heats the blade of her knife. She cuts the umbilical cord. Together the two women sleep, Ela holding her new baby on her chest.

Again the night cold comes, but under the tree they are cosy. Lozen thanks the tree for her shelter.

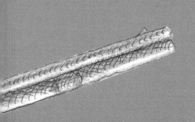

The next day, the women began the long journey across the desert to the Mescalero Apache Reservation to join the rest of their people. It takes them weeks. They hid from soldiers and settlers. Lozen stole two horses so she and Ela could cross the vast lands. When they finally arrived they learned that Lozen's brother, Victorio, had escaped the United States Cavalry only to be ambushed by Mexican forces. He and many of his warriors died. Hearing this terrible news, Lozen joined the great Apache Warrior, Geronimo, and continued the fight.

Elizabeth

THE STOIC PRINCESS

In England, around 500 years ago, Elizabeth was accused of betraying the Queen who was her own sister …

Elizabeth rolls the idea around her mind like a marble in a bowl.

"If they had proof, they would have chopped off my head. I still have my head. So they have no proof," she thinks to herself.

The young princess is sitting on a wooden stool. Across the table sit seven old men in large chairs with plush cushions. By the light of the blazing fire, they take notes of everything she says. They are trying to trap her with her own words. They ask her question after question. They are trying to exhaust her, make her confess.

The oldest man growls angrily, "How many times have we asked you this question?"

"Forgive me, Bishop Gardiner," Elizabeth replies.
"I don't know exactly, but we have spoken daily for
the two weeks that I have been in the Tower."

Sweat forms on her brow. It trickles down her hairline.

Bishop Gardiner's eyes harden. Like a snake, he has no
eyelashes. He takes a sip from his goblet. No drink is
given to Elizabeth.

The bishop wants Elizabeth dead, and she knows the
complicated reasons why. If her sister doesn't have a
baby then Elizabeth will inherit the throne.

Elizabeth is loyal to the new church, but Bishop
Gardiner believes in the old ways, the Catholic Church.
Her sister, Queen Mary, is Catholic so the bishop is
devoted to her. Outside these prison walls there is a
conspiracy to overthrow the Catholic queen and make
Elizabeth queen.

One of the men at the table mutters to the bishop,
"Every traitor brags about how young Princess Elizabeth
will replace her own sister, our beloved Queen Mary.
Yet she denies all knowledge of the plot. Impossible."

The bishop turns sharply on Elizabeth. "I cannot rack
you. Do you know what the rack is? How we tie the
person to it? And turn the wheel?"

Elizabeth knows the rack breaks bones.

"Thomas Wyatt," says the bishop, his snake eyes
gleaming. "He dared to march on London with 3,000
men and carry out his plan to put you on the throne, but
the people did not join his rebellion. We captured him,

Elizabeth hits back with short, honest answers.

put him on the rack. His trial is finished. He is guilty. He will be executed, but not yet … He has more to tell – more to tell about you."

Elizabeth listens, as still as a painting.

"He tells us that you knew of the rebellion against Queen Mary, that you begged him to make you queen."

Elizabeth narrows her eyes in thought. "This is a lie. If Thomas Wyatt said this I would already be dead."

The bishop slashes at her with more questions. "When did you meet the traitor Thomas? Did you know his father? What about the other conspirators?"

Elizabeth hits back with short, honest answers. It is too difficult to remember lies when she is asked so many questions at such speed.

As fast as the questions and answers come, the men in black scratch each word on their paper with their quivering quills.

The bishop grins. In a voice like syrup he asks a question that seems easier to answer, "Do you like your room? It is fit for a queen."

The princess lowers her head to hide the distress on her face. The bishop smirks. He is so excited, he claps his hands together in a quiet flutter of applause.

Elizabeth was grateful when she first saw her room, her place of imprisonment. It is larger than this hot room in which she now sits being questioned. Her room is not a dungeon cell, but a gracious bedroom with three windows, a comfortable bed and a large fireplace. Down the hall are toilets that empty into the moat.

But her gratitude did not last long. She soon learned the bishop's cruel scheme. He had locked her in the same room where her mother had been imprisoned and awaited her execution.

Everyone in England knows that Elizabeth's mother was executed, and that the order was given by her father.

The bishop asks her again, "Do you like your room?"

Elizabeth clenches her jaw.

The bishop bangs the table, yells, demands her answer. "Do you like your room?"

The other councillors jump.

Elizabeth recovers and answers simply, "Yes."

Then, from the other side of the locked wooden door, comes an even louder BANG, BANG, BANG!

The bishop twists round. "Who has the right to interrupt me?" He stomps to the door, opening it a crack.

The man behind the door bellows, "You think I am a fool, Bishop Gardiner? Look at this death warrant! This rubbish warrant comes from you and your schemers on the Queen's council! It has no seal! No signature!"

Elizabeth closes her eyes as shouting continues.

"You think you can trick me into killing the sister of the queen without the Queen's signature?"

The bishop coos, "No, not without a signature. Shh – she is here now. Let's discuss this later ... Nobody could trick you ... "

The bishop finally convinces the angry man to leave. Elizabeth opens her eyes.

The bishop politely excuses the interruption. "A small problem with your warrant."

Elizabeth responds coolly. "Yes, a signature is small. Small, but important." Her voice is steady and she even manages a small smile, as though they are discussing nothing more serious than dropping a sewing stitch.

Rage surges through the bishop.

"You know who that man is?" he snarls. "He oversees all the executions! He organised the execution of your cousin Lady Jane Grey – dead. Lord Dudley – dead. Thomas Wyatt – about to die. And you? Tell me who he is!"

Elizabeth's dry mouth mutters, "The Lieutenant of the Tower."

The Bishop laughs. "Yes. You already know him. That is good. You wouldn't want to meet for the first time when he … " He pauses, willing Elizabeth to imagine her own death.

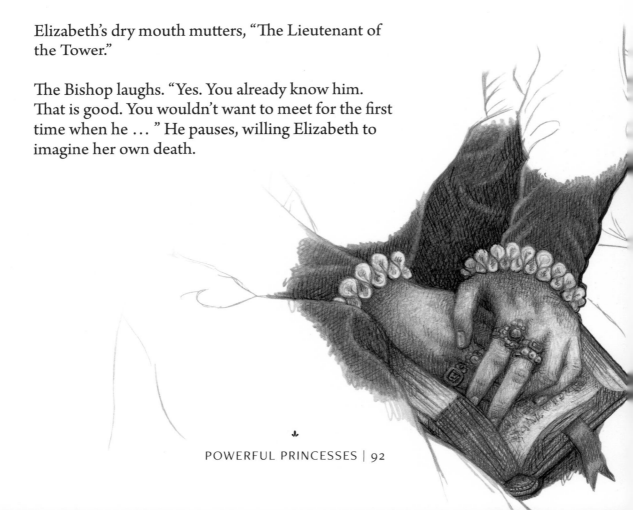

Elizabeth retorts, "You don't have a signature on that death warrant. My sister, Queen Mary, has not signed my death warrant."

"YET! She has not signed it yet!" snaps the Bishop.

Elizabeth forces herself to be calm. "We all have to be careful here. Executing the wrong person can lead to one's own execution. You wouldn't want to make a mistake, Bishop Gardiner. You too have been imprisoned in the Tower."

He bares his teeth like a savage dog. "But we have the letters! Traitor Thomas wrote to you of his rebellion!"

Elizabeth is obstinate. "I never received any letter."

"Your servant says you did receive the letter. He saw you holding it, reading it! You answered – that you would do as God demanded."

Elizabeth feels sick. She remembers that letter. The letter.

It was months ago. The rider, who carried the letter, came to her home on a grey winter day.

"The letter!" the bishop screams in her face.

When Elizabeth first read the scrawling ink message she felt fear. She guessed it had been read by the Queen's spies before reaching her. She did not write back to the rebels, but why hadn't she warned the Queen?

A tiny voice inside Elizabeth whispers, "The bishop is right. I was a traitor to my own sister."

Meanwhile, the bishop yells on and on. "Traitor, traitor, traitor – the letter proves you are a traitor!"

Elizabeth ignores the shouting and the flying spit of the red-faced bishop. Rather, she wrestles with her conscience, thinking, "My sister. It is these men who set us against each other. Yes, she is seventeen years older than me and we don't share a mother, but she is my sister and my queen. I should have told her about the letter. But I will not die for that mistake. I will not die."

With fierce control, Elizabeth lies, "I never received the letter. Never."

The bishop drives on. "We have another letter! Traitor Thomas wrote to the French ambassador – that you support his rebellion! You will organise troops!"

This is a shock for Elizabeth. She pinches the soft skin of her arm to stay focussed. "So, what is your question?"

"You supported treason against your sister, our Majesty, Queen Mary!"

Now Elizabeth is confident in the truth.

"I know nothing of this letter. I am not responsible for other men's words. I raised no army. I am no traitor."

The bishop hurls his goblet at the princess. She swerves. It clatters to the stone floor.

Elizabeth stares at the bishop's hot, swollen face.

"Take her back to her room. Walk her past the scaffold on the way. We will meet again tomorrow."

The bishop retreats from the room.

Elizabeth sighs. She has won; won another day.
She needs to win tomorrow and the next day.
But every little victory is keeping her alive.
"You will not trick me. I will live."

And win she did. Princess Elizabeth was kept in the Tower for two terrifying months, but she survived to become the Queen of England. She ruled for 45 years with the strength she proved during those long interrogations.